CRITTER CRACKERS

THE ABC BOOK OF LIMERICKS

written and illustrated by

KATHRYN BARRON

LANDMARK EDITIONS, INC.

P.O. Box 4469   1402 Kansas Avenue   Kansas City, Missouri 64127

(816) 241-4919

Dedicated to
my little brother Mark,
who likes to watch me draw,
and to the memory of my
"adopted grandpa," Donald McLean,
who loved a good poem.

International Standard Book Number: 0-933849-58-3 (LIB.BDG.)

Library of Congress Cataloging-in-Publication Data
Barron, Kathryn, 1980-
   Critter crackers : the ABC book of limericks /
written and illustrated by Kathryn Barron.
   p. cm.
   Summary: A collection of limericks each of which describes an
animal whose name begins with a different letter of the alphabet.
   ISBN 0-933849-58-3 (lib.bdg. : acid-free paper)
   1. Children's poetry.   2. Animals—Juvenile poetry.
   3. Limericks.   4. Alphabet rhymes.
   [1. Limericks. 2. Animals—Poetry. 3. Poetry. 4. Alphabet.]

   I. Title.
PS3552.A73697C75   1995
811'.54—dc20—dc20
[[E]]
                                95-8700
                                CIP
                                AC

Editorial Coordinator: Nancy R. Thatch
Creative Coordinator: David Melton
Production Assistant: Brian Hubbard

Printed in the United States of America

Landmark Editions, Inc.
P.O. Box 4469
1402 Kansas Avenue
Kansas City, Missouri 64127
(816) 241-4919

CRITTER CRACKERS
The ABC Book of Limericks

Anyone who thinks it is easy to create a good alphabet book has probably never tried to create one. Good alphabet books are very difficult to develop, because they usually have no overall plot or story, and they do not contain one central character.

There are 26 letters in the English language, so alphabet books are automatically divided into 26 parts. Those 26 letters are always presented in the same sequence — *alphabetically* from A to Z.

To delight and surprise the reader and viewer, the author/illustrator must address all 26 letters without running out of fresh ideas along the way, insuring that X, Y, and Z maintain the same vibrant energy of A, B, and C. As you are about to discover, Kathryn Barron has met the challenge and triumphed. For each letter of the alphabet in CRITTER CRACKERS, she has created a witty limerick with clever plays on words and twists on thoughts that never become commonplace nor trite.

Kathryn's colorful illustrations are terrific, too. The characters she has created are delightful to look at, and she has skillfully composed her scenes to capture the critters' actions at just the right moments.

Kathryn is fun to work with! She is quick-witted and has a wonderful sense of humor. She always seemed to appreciate the help and suggestions editor Nan Thatch and I offered for her limericks and her art. By the same token, we developed an appreciation for Kathryn, her talents, her skills, and her dedication to improving her work.

Now — if you are ready to have a lot of fun with CRITTER CRACKERS from A to Z, just turn the page.

— David Melton
Creative Coordinator
Landmark Editions, Inc.

There's a big alligator named Al,
Who lives by a swampy canal.
If you see him grin,
Then he's taken you in,
For gators *love* lunch with a pal!

B

There once was a beaver named Lee,
Who thought he could eat a whole tree.
He began at the bottom,
But it toppled and got him.
Now his tail is as flat as can be!

A camel in Kalamazoo
Served tea to the Sheik of Shamoo.
With politeness extreme,
She'd ask, "Sugar or cream?"
And then, "Is that one hump or two?"

A clever young dolphin named Dwight
Likes to search in the ocean at night.
Of the dark he's not scared,
'Cause he swims well prepared
With a high-powered, waterproof light.

An elephant said, "I suppose
Some people make fun of my nose.
    But on hot summer days,
    I cool off in its sprays,
'Cause my trunk doubles up as a hose."

Freddy the Frog was unwise;
He was tired of eating just flies.
    So he tasted some bees,
        Then he gasped and he wheezed —
Their stingers were quite a surprise!

A goofy gorilla named Lou
Entertains all the folks at the zoo.
    As they giggle and grin,
        And say, "Look at HIM!"
He turns back and laughs, "Look at YOU!"

A spiny old hedgehog named Pickles
Admired his beautiful stickles.
"I've got spines and not fuzz,
And I'm laughing because
When I roll myself up, it sure tickles!"

A cute little inchworm named Porter
Was always the kid who was shorter.
Then one day by a fence,
He found twenty-five cents,
And now he's an inch and a quarter!

I know a swift jaguar named Jim,
Who's speedy, and wiry, and slim.
When he whizzes past,
He's going so fast
That his spots can't keep up with him.

There once was a lost kangaroo,
Whose mother cried out, "Where are you?"
  Said his dad, "Try your pocket;
  This key should unlock it."
And Joey popped out — PEEK-A-BOO!

A fearless young lion named Wayne
Was prowling outside in the rain.
A lightning bolt hit him;
Like a light bulb it lit him.
Now he has an electrified mane!

M

A Mexican mouse named José
Ate hot chili peppers all day.
He heaped his plate higher,
'Til his breath caught on fire,
And he toasted his whiskers away!

Nigel, a negligent newt,
Misplaced his mother's gold flute.
　　It was found near the stairs
　　In a jar of canned pears,
In the sleeve of his father's best suit.

A little opossum said, "Whee!
I can swing by my tail from a tree!
The ground is the sky,
And the grass is up high.
Now *this* is how nature should be!"

A hungry old pigeon named Mark
Ate popcorn and nuts in the park.
  Before he exploded,
  He was tied up and loaded
To his home by three crows and a lark.

Quincy, a sea-going quail,
Was sailing to France in a pail.
He got sick from the motion
And fell in the ocean,
And was carried to shore by a whale.

Ricky, a ring-tailed raccoon,
Ate ice cream on a hot afternoon.
The ice cream got squishy,
And Ricky sure wished he
Had snacked by the light of the moon.

S

A silly old serpent named Vance
Was invited to go to a dance.
He spent fifty bucks
And rented a tux,
But he couldn't fit into the pants!

T

A man-eating tiger named Thor
Broke right through the walls of a store.
But there was no panic in
Stalking a manikin —
Hunting dummies was really a bore!

u

In rain the umbrella bird sloshes;
In puddles she splashes and sploshes.
Her umbrella's so high,
Her feet won't stay dry,
So she keeps them inside her galoshes.

Vanessa the Vulture sighed, "Oh!
I'm not pretty like Carol the Crow."
Said her mother, "Don't weep,
Beauty's just feather-deep.
You're the prettiest vulture I know!"

I know of a walrus named Willy,
Whose fear of the water is silly.
 On his iceberg he blubbers
 With other landlubbers.
He says that the water's too chilly.

A creature beginning with "X"
Has left me completely perplexed.
 I can't think of many;
 I'm not sure there's *any*;
So let's just go on to the next...

Y

Yogi, a talkative yak,
Talked 'til his friends hollered, "Ack!
 If you don't shut your mouth,
  You'll be known north and south
As *Yogi the Yackety-Yak*!"

Z

There once was a zebra named Zay,
Whose stripes all had vanished away.
    And now he has lots
      Of pink polka dots,
Of which he is proud, I must say.

Karen Kerber
age 12

David McAdoo
age 14

Amy Hagstrom
age 9

Isaac Whitlatch
age 11

Michael Cain
age 11

Amity Gaige
age 16

Adam Moore
age 9

Ben Kendall
age 7

Steven Shepard
age 13

Travis Williams
age 16

by Karen Kerber, age 12
St. Louis, Missouri
A delightfully playful book! The text is loaded with clever alliterations and gentle humor. Karen's brightly colored illustrations are composed of wiggly and waggly strokes of genius.
Printed Full Color
ISBN 0-933849-29-X $14.95

by David McAdoo, age 14
Springfield, Missouri
An exciting intergalactic adventure! In the distant future, a courageous warrior defends a kingdom from a dragon from outer space. Astounding sepia illustrations.
Printed Duotone
ISBN 0-933849-23-0 $14.95

by Amy Hagstrom, age 9
Portola, California
An exciting western! When a boy and an old Indian try to save a herd of wild ponies, they discover a lost canyon and see the mystical vision of the Great White Stallion.
Printed Full Color
ISBN 0-933849-15-X $14.95

by Isaac Whitlatch, age 11
Casper, Wyoming
The true confessions of a devo etable hater! Isaac tells ways to and dispose of the "slimy things." His colorful illustratio vide a salad of laughter and mi
Printed Full Color
ISBN 0-933849-16-8 $1

by Michael Cain, age 11
Annapolis, Maryland
A glorious tale of adventure! To become a knight, a young man must face a beast in the forest, a spell-binding witch, and a giant bird that guards a magic oval crystal.
Printed Full Color
ISBN 0-933849-26-5 $14.95

by Amity Gaige, age 16
Reading, Pennsylvania
A lyrical blend of poetry and photographs! Amity's sensitive poems offer thought-provoking ideas and amusing insights. This lovely book is one to be savored and enjoyed.
Printed Full Color
ISBN 0-933849-27-3 $14.95

by Adam Moore, age 9
Broken Arrow, Oklahoma
A remarkable true story! When Adam was eight years old, he fell and ran an arrow into his head. With rare insight and humor, he tells of his ordeal and his amazing recovery.
Printed Two Colors
ISBN 0-933849-24-9 $14.95

by Michael Aushenker, age 19
Ithaca, New York
Chomp! Chomp! When Arth gets to feed his goat, the anim everything in sight. A very funn –good to the last bite. The i tions are terrific.
Printed Full Color
ISBN 0-933849-28-1 $1

SPECIAL NOTICE

You Too May Become a Published Author

If you are 6 to 19 years of age, you may write and illustrate a wonderful book and enter it in the Contest.

To obtain a free copy of the Contest Rules and Guidelines, send a self-addressed, business-size envelope, stamped with .64 cents postage to:
The National Written & Illustrated by...
Awards Contest
Landmark Editions, Inc.
1402 Kansas Avenue
Kansas City, Missouri 64127

by Benjamin Kendall, age 7
State College, Pennsylvania
When Ben wears his new super-hero costume, he sees Aliens who are from outer space. His attempts to stop the pesky invaders provide loads of laughs. Colorful drawings add to the fun!
Printed Full Color
ISBN 0-933849-42-7 $14.95

by Steven Shepard, age 13
Great Falls, Virginia
A gripping thriller! When a boy rows his boat to an island to retrieve a stolen knife, he faces threatening fog, treacherous currents, and a sinister lobsterman. Outstanding drawings!
Printed Full Color
ISBN 0-933849-43-5

by Travis Williams, age 16
Sardis, B.C., Canada
A chilling mystery! When a teen discovers his classmates are mis becomes entrapped in a web of ing stories, false alibis, and frig changes. Dramatic drawings!
Printed Two Color
ISBN 0-933849-44-3 $1

Students and Adults Enjoy All the Winning Books!

Leslie A MacKeen
age 9

Elizabeth Haidle
age 13

Heidi Salter
age 19

Lauren Peters
age 7

Jayna Miller
age 19

Alise Leggatt
age 8

Lisa Butenhoff
age 13

Shintaro Maeda
age 8

Miles MacGregor
age 12

Kristin Pedersen
age 18

by Leslie Ann MacKeen, age 9
Winston-Salem, North Carolina
Loaded with fun and puns! When Jeremiah T. Fitz's car stops running, several animals offer suggestions for fixing it. The results are hilarious. The illustrations are charming.
Printed Full Color
ISBN 0-933849-19-2 $14.95

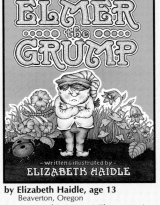

by Elizabeth Haidle, age 13
Beaverton, Oregon
A very touching story! The grumpiest Elfkin learns to cherish the friendship of others after he helps an injured snail and befriends an orphaned boy. Absolutely beautiful.
Printed Full Color
ISBN 0-933849-20-6 $14.95

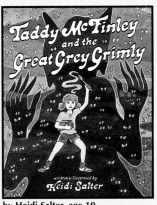

by Heidi Salter, age 19
Berkeley, California
Spooky and wonderful! To save her vivid imagination, a young girl must confront the Great Grey Grimly himself. The narrative is filled with suspense. Vibrant illustrations.
Printed Full Color
ISBN 0-933849-21-4 $14.95

by Lauren Peters, age 7
Kansas City, Missouri
The Christmas that almost w[asn't]. When Santa Claus takes a va[cation], Mrs. Claus and the elves go on [strike]. Toys aren't made. Cookies [aren't] baked. Super illustrations.
Printed Full Color
ISBN 0-933849-25-7 $1[4.95]

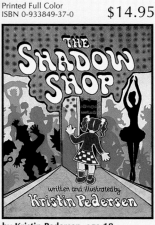

by Jayna Miller, age 19
Zanesville, Ohio
The funniest Halloween ever! When Jammer the Rabbit takes all the treats, his friends get even. Their hilarious scheme includes a haunted house and mounds of chocolate.
Printed Full Color
ISBN 0-933849-37-0 $14.95

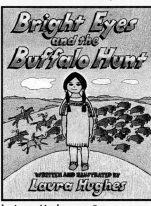

by Alise Leggat, age 8
Culpepper, Virginia
Amy J. Kendrick wants to play football, but her mother wants her to become a ballerina. Their clash of wills creates hilarious situations. Clever, delightful illustrations.
Printed Full Color
ISBN 0-933849-39-7 $14.95

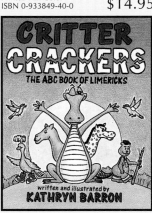

by Lisa Kirsten Butenhoff, age 13
Woodbury, Minnesota
The people of a Russian Village face the winter without warm clothes or enough food. Then their lives are improved by a young girl's gifts. A tender story with lovely illustrations.
Printed Full Color
ISBN 0-933849-40-0 $14.95

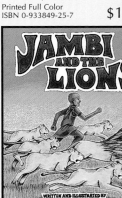

by Jennifer Brady, age 17
Columbia, Missouri
When poachers capture a pr[ide of] lions, a native boy tries to free t[he ani]mals. A skillfully told story. G[reat] illustrations illuminate this [African] adventure.
Printed Full Color
ISBN 0-933849-41-9 $1[4.95]

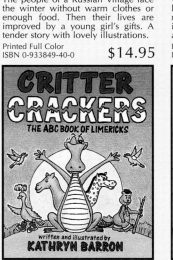

by Kristin Pedersen, age 18
Etobicoke, Ont., Canada
A mysterious parable, told in rhyme. When Thelma McMurty trades her shadow, she thinks she will live happily ever after. But an old gypsy knows better. The collage illustrations are brilliant!
Printed Full Color
ISBN 0-933849-53-2 $14.95

by Laura Hughes, age 8
Woonsocket, Rhode Island
When a Dakota Indian girl finds a herd of buffalo, the big hunt of the year begins! An exciting fiction-based-on-fact story with wonderful illustrations that younger children will enjoy.
Printed Full Color
ISBN 0-933849-57-5 $14.95

by Kathryn Barron, age 13
Emo, Ont., Canada
Funny from A to Z! Kathryn's hilarious limericks and delightfully witty illustrations provide laughs, page after page! An absolutely charming book for young children.
Printed Full Color
ISBN 0-933849-58-3 $14.95

by Taramesha Maniatty, age 1[7]
Morrisville, Vermont
A young man is determined that h[is] sledding team will win the race. In l[os]ing the competition, he is forced t[o make] the most difficult decision of [his life]. Brilliant text and paintings.
Printed Full Color
ISBN 0-933849-59-1 $1[4.95]

All BOOKS FOR STUDENTS BY STUDENTS® are 29 pages, printed on 100-pound, acid-free paper. They have laminated hardcovers and reinforced library bindings for added durability.